SYMBOLS OF SALVATION
DAILY DEVOTIONS

Aretta Gordish

CONCORDIA PUBLISHING HOUSE · SAINT LOUIS

Read It Again!

Sing to the LORD, bless His name; tell of His
salvation from day to day.

Psalm 96:2

When my children were little, they each had a favorite book they wanted me to read over and over again. If I was in a hurry and left out some of the details, they would stop me and make me go back and reread the page. After I finished the story, they would often say, "Mommy, read it again!"

The account of Christ's birth is much like that. We never grow tired of hearing it. Each year at Advent and Christmas, we look to the familiar passages in God's Word and once again find joy in that awe-inspiring story of how the Word became flesh and dwelt among us (John 1:14). This true story of salvation has been shared not only from year to year but also from generation to generation.

Even long before Jesus was born, God foretold of Christ's birth to the prophets of old. Now here we are, thousands of years after Christ's birth, still saying, "Read it again!" We want to hear about the One who came to set us free! It's a story so wonderful that you want to hear and tell it over and over again.

Heavenly Father, as we begin this season of Advent, may the familiar story of Jesus' birth rekindle in us the hope we have in Your salvation as we wait for Your promised return. In Jesus' name we pray. Amen.

O Little Town of Bethlehem

But you, O Bethlehem Ephrathah, who are too little to
be among the clans of Judah, from you shall come forth
for me one who is to be ruler in Israel, whose coming
forth is from of old, from ancient days.

Micah 5:2

With eyes as big as saucers, a child beholds all the gifts under the Christmas tree and wonders which one he should open first. I don't know about you, but when I was a child, I always wanted to open the biggest present first, thinking it would be the best gift of all. So often, we assume that bigger is better, but that's not always the case. Some of the costliest gifts are found in little packages.

We read in the Book of Micah that the town of Bethlehem was so little it wasn't even considered among the clans of Judah. It was just a little dot on the map, and yet from this location, something huge was going to happen. Hundreds of years before Christ's birth, it was foretold that a ruler would be born in this little town of Bethlehem. He was not just any ruler, though. This baby, born in this little town, would come to be our most precious gift: the Savior who would take away the sin of the world.

O Holy Child of Bethlehem, descend to us we pray; cast out our sin
and enter in, be born in us today. (*LSB* 361:4)

Born of a Virgin

Therefore the Lord Himself will give you a sign.
Behold, the virgin shall conceive and bear a son,
and shall call His name Immanuel.

Isaiah 7:14

No matter where you go, even in a different country, there will be signs posted here and there to give people directions to exits or, more importantly, restrooms. Signs also help keep you and those around you safe while you're driving. Watching carefully for stop or yield signs can help you avoid being in a major accident. Signs are important, but sadly, not everyone follows them. We still hear about people getting injured or even dying because they simply ignored the signs.

God, who loves us so dearly, gave us a sign. He wanted to make sure that we recognized the Savior He was sending, so He promised us the sign that our Savior would be born of a virgin. It would be a miraculous birth, so amazing that we would surely see and know that this truly was the Son of God, sent to abide with us and to save us from our sin.

Many have ignored the signs and still live in darkness. But God loves the world and is patiently waiting for all to follow the signs that will lead them to Jesus Christ.

Heavenly Father, we pray that You would cast all doubt and fear away, so that we may clearly see the way that leads to everlasting life. In Jesus' name. Amen.

Good News

The Spirit of the Lord God is upon Me, because the
Lord has anointed Me to bring good news to the
poor; He has sent Me to bind up the brokenhearted, to
proclaim liberty to the captives, and the opening of the
prison to those who are bound.

Isaiah 61:1

A consequence is something that logically follows from an action or condition. If you study hard for a test, a good grade should follow. If you go outside without your coat on during a snowstorm, you will be cold. If you save money, your bank account will grow; but if you rob a bank, you're looking at many years of prison time. Good or bad, no matter how hard you try, you can't avoid the consequences of your actions.

The natural consequence of our sin was death. It was what we deserved, and it seemed as if that was exactly what we were going to get . . . or was it? God had some good news to share with a hurting world. He was sending His Son to earth to heal our brokenness and to set us free from the consequences of our sin, so that we might have life eternal. It is incomprehensible that anyone could love someone so much, and yet that is exactly how much God loves us. This is indeed very good news.

Heavenly Father, in a world full of sad news, we are grateful for the good news that You came to set us free from sin. In Jesus' name. Amen.

For This Purpose

Now is My soul troubled. And what shall I say?
"Father, save Me from this hour"? But for this purpose
I have come to this hour.

John 12:27

On this, the Second Sunday in Advent, you may be starting to feel the "hustle and bustle" of the season. You're excited, but you're also starting to feel stressed by the things you still need to get done. You have trees to trim, parties to attend, and all those presents to wrap.

Or you might be dreading the sadness and loneliness that so many struggle with this time of year. Those in the military who are deployed to a foreign land are longing to be home. Those who have recently lost a spouse may not want to celebrate without their loved one near. Those who have lost a job may be wondering if there will be any gifts at all this year.

Wherever you are in life this season, remember that the purpose for celebrating Christ's birth is not about gifts or being with loved ones. Yes, those things are nice, but even without them, we still have reason to celebrate. Jesus came with the sole purpose of sacrificing His life for ours. We can still celebrate with joy in our hearts, knowing that we are now free from the burden of sin.

Heavenly Father, may we celebrate the birth of Your Son with joy as we reflect on the purpose for which He came. In His name we pray. Amen.

The Grace of God

For the grace of God has appeared,
bringing salvation for all people.

Titus 2:11

Grace is one of those words that is not easily defined. One dictionary had seventeen different meanings. For example, in one definition, it means approval, as in being in one's good graces. Other meanings include favor, pardon, a privilege, or even how one might address a duke or duchess. It's also what we call the short prayer we say at mealtimes.

Still another definition of *grace* is a reprieve, a release or deliverance, freedom from liability.

This definition well describes the grace of God. He knew that the world was in dire need of a Savior. God, who loves His people, revealed to them that a Savior would be born who would take away the sin of the world. He was sending us a reprieve from the punishment we all deserve because of our sin.

The grace of God brought salvation to all people. It reprieved us from the punishment we deserved. God's grace appeared to us to set us free from our sin. It appeared to us to save us from death. It appeared to us in the person of Jesus Christ, God's only-begotten Son. It is a free gift for all those who believe.

Gracious heavenly Father, we thank You for the salvation You freely give to all people. Open our eyes and ears, so that we may believe in all You foretold to us about our Savior, Jesus Christ. In His name. Amen.

Still with Us

All this took place to fulfill what the Lord had spoken
by the prophet: "Behold, the virgin shall conceive and
bear a son, and they shall call His name Immanuel"
(which means, God with us).

Matthew 1:22–23

There was a law in the Old Testament that required the men to appear before the Lord three times during the year. They were also not to appear empty-handed but were to give according to the blessings they had been given (Deuteronomy 16:16–17). How difficult that must have been for these men. Transportation was usually by foot back in that day, so they had to travel for days, if not weeks, to fulfill this law.

To hear that God was sending His Son, Immanuel, must have given the people so much hope. They would no longer have to appear before the Lord three times a year, for the Lord was coming and would appear before them. He did not appear empty-handed either. He brought with Him an abundance of blessings and gifts. He came to teach, to heal, but most importantly, to save them from their sin and their inability to fulfill the Law.

Immanuel indeed has come and has promised that He is still with us through the power of the Holy Spirit, who dwells within us.

Thank You, heavenly Father, that You are always with us. Continue to lead, guide, and teach us the ways that lead to righteousness. In Jesus' name we pray. Amen.

Keep Guard

By the Holy Spirit who dwells within us, guard the
good deposit entrusted to you.

2 Timothy 1:14

Many of us have a lockbox where we keep important papers or expensive items. We also may put in security systems with alarms to scare off those who would try to take our treasures. We want to hold on to the things we have, so we keep guard over them.

When God sent His Son, Jesus, to earth, He did so for the purpose of bringing us salvation. Christ suffered and died to bring this treasure to us. He rose from the dead to give us victory over death. When Jesus ascended into heaven, God sent His Holy Spirit to dwell within us so He would always be with us. There is no treasure greater than this precious gift of salvation entrusted to us, but there is one who persistently schemes to take it from us.

However, the Holy Spirit, who dwells within us, is the best security system for keeping our treasures protected from the evil one. He will help us guard what has been entrusted to us. He will give us strength to fight off the one who is constantly trying to take it from us. We can rest easy at night, knowing that God never sleeps and is always keeping guard over us.

Heavenly Father, You have entrusted us with a gift more precious than gold. Help us treasure this gracious gift. In Jesus' name we pray. Amen.

For This Reason

For this reason I bow my knees before the Father.

Ephesians 3:14

There is a catchy phrase this time of year: "Jesus is the reason for the season." It's a reminder to us to take our eyes off the things of this world and to turn our eyes toward Jesus. In doing so, we may be surprised to learn that actually, *you and I* are the reason for the season.

When God sent His Son to be born, it was for our salvation. God wasn't doing it for Jesus. Jesus wasn't in need of a Savior; we were! After Jesus had already returned to heaven, Paul wrote to the Ephesians, letting them know that he had been brought to his knees as he earnestly prayed for them. He wanted them to understand the reason Jesus came. He wanted them to be strengthened by the Holy Spirit that had been sent to dwell within them. He wanted them to be filled with the fullness of God and to know His love (Ephesians 3:14–20).

This same message is one that should also bring us to our knees as we pray for all those who have not yet heard the good news that we are the reason for the season.

Heavenly Father, help us to always remember the reason that You came. Give us courage to gladly share it with others, so that they too may put their trust in You. In Jesus' name we pray. Amen.

God's Temple

Do you not know that you are God's temple
and that God's Spirit dwells in you?

1 Corinthians 3:16

Jean Anthelme Brillat-Savarin was not a chef, but he enjoyed writing about food. He once said, "Tell me what you eat, and I will tell you what you are." Later, this phrase was shortened to "You are what you eat." Basically, if you want to be healthy and fit, you need to eat healthy foods. That may be hard to remember with all our holiday baking!

This concept of "you are what you eat" is true of our spiritual life as well. You see, God is no longer dwelling in a temple made of stone; His Spirit now dwells in you. What do you eat when you are the temple of the living God? Jesus shared the recipe to keep us spiritually healthy and strong. "Man shall not live by bread alone, but by every word that comes from the mouth of God" (Matthew 4:4).

We need to remain steadfast in God's Word, knowing He is dwelling within us. We rejoice in knowing He has promised to come again and bring us to where He is, so that we may dwell with Him in heaven forever and ever.

Heavenly Father, it is humbling to know that we are the temple for Your Spirit. May we daily be reminded of this as we feast upon the good food You provide for us in Your Holy Word. In Jesus' name we pray. Amen.

Giver of Life

If the Spirit of Him who raised Jesus from the dead
dwells in you, He who raised Christ Jesus from the
dead will also give life to your mortal bodies through
His Spirit who dwells in you.

Romans 8:11

An interesting poll taken in 2019 asked people how afraid they were of death: 11 percent were very afraid, 31 percent were somewhat afraid, 27 percent were not very afraid, 25 percent were not afraid at all, and less than 7 percent didn't know. It is fair to say that, according to these statistics, most people have some fear of death.

Jesus suffered greatly as He hung and died upon a cross. After three days, women went to the tomb and found it empty and were afraid. Angels appeared and reminded them that Jesus had foretold that though He would die, He would also rise again (Luke 24:7). This same Spirit who raised Jesus from the dead dwells in all of us who believe that He truly is the Son of God. This same Spirit dwelling in us will also give life to our mortal bodies. We do not need to fear death, for we have been given life eternal.

Heavenly Father, so often we forget that You are the giver of life. Forgive us when our doubt causes us to fear. In Jesus' name we pray. Amen.

Came to Destroy

Whoever makes a practice of sinning is of the devil,
for the devil has been sinning from the beginning. The
reason the Son of God appeared was to destroy the
works of the devil.

1 John 3:8

Today is the Third Sunday in Advent, also called Gaudete Sunday. In Latin, *Gaudete* means "rejoice." It's hard to think about rejoicing when we hear of sin and the devil as we do in our Scripture verse today. However, we can, and should, rejoice in knowing that Jesus came to destroy sin and the devil.

In the Book of Genesis, we see the devil begin his long history of lying to and deceiving mankind. God had clearly stated that eating from the tree of life would bring death, but the devil lied and stated, "You will not surely die" (Genesis 3:4). The devil still lies to each of us in hopes that we will continue to make a habit of our sin. But God, who never lies, really did say that sin leads to death.

Thankfully, God sent Jesus to destroy the works of the devil, which He did successfully as He hung upon the cross, paying the price we should have paid for our sins. He then rose from the dead, victorious over sin, death, the devil, and all the devil's evil ways, fully accomplishing what He came to do. Indeed, this is cause to rejoice.

Heavenly Father, help us to recognize our sin, to turn away from it, and to follow You with grateful hearts full of rejoicing in all Your ways. In Jesus' name we pray. Amen.

He Dwells in You

In Him you also are being built together into a
dwelling place for God by the Spirit.

Ephesians 2:22

The ark of the covenant is described in the Bible in Exodus 25. God gave Moses very clear instructions on how to build it. He then told Moses about the mercy seat, the part of the ark from which God would communicate with him and give him all the commands for the Israelites. The people knew that the ark was a sacred thing in which God Himself dwelled among His people.

No one knows for certain what happened to the ark of the covenant. We do know, however, that God no longer dwells within it. He dwells in you and in everyone who believes in His Son, Jesus Christ. 1 John 4:15 states this: "Whoever confesses that Jesus is the Son of God, God abides in him, and he in God."

The season of Advent is a time of anticipation of the celebration of Christ's birth, but it's also a time of waiting for the Lord's promised return. It is a time of remembering the promise that we will one day dwell with God in heaven. Until then, we are comforted in knowing that He dwells within us through the power of the Holy Spirit.

O Lord, we are grateful that You are always with us. In life, You abide with us, and in death, You are still there and will raise us again to live and dwell with You in heaven. In Jesus' blessed name we pray. Amen.

Humbled Even to Death

But we see Him who for a little while was made lower
than the angels, namely Jesus, crowned with glory and
honor because of the suffering of death, so that by the
grace of God He might taste death for everyone.

Hebrews 2:9

Vincent de Paul was a priest who lived during the 1600s. He once said, "The most powerful weapon to conquer the devil is humility. For, as he does not know at all how to employ it, neither does he know how to defend himself from it." From Jesus' lowly birth to His cruel death upon a cross, we see that Jesus' humility was indeed a very powerful weapon.

The devil tried everything he could to prevent Jesus from accomplishing what God had sent Him to do. After Jesus had fasted for forty days, the devil used his cunning deception to tempt Jesus to bow down before him, but he was powerless in the face of humility. Though Jesus was King of all, He was striped and beaten, humbled even to death upon a cross. But again, the devil would not succeed. Death could not hold Jesus in the grave. He rose again victorious, no longer humbled.

Though Jesus was made low for just a little while, He is now high and lifted up and will reign forever and ever, crowned with glory and honor.

Heavenly Father, we humbly bow before You and give You thanks
and praise for taking our place on the cross. In Jesus' name. Amen.

Foolish, Weak, Low, and Despised

But God chose what is foolish in the world to shame
the wise; God chose what is weak in the world to
shame the strong; God chose what is low and despised
in the world, even things that are not, to bring to
nothing things that are, so that no human being might
boast in the presence of God.

1 Corinthians 1:27–29

Throughout the Bible, God uses the foolish, weak, low, and despised to bring down haughty warriors and arrogant kings. A young shepherd boy who trusts in God is able to kill a nine-foot warrior. As foolish as it seemed, three young men would not obey the order to bow down to a golden image. Though they were thrown into a furnace, they trusted God, and not a hair on their head was singed. The once-boastful king declared that no one could ever speak against their God.

What the world deems foolish, God sees as an opportunity to reveal His glory. Though Jesus should have entered the world with a royal fanfare, God chose that He should be born among stable animals. He was despised to the point of death. However, one day, all will see His glory. When He returns, "every knee [will] bow . . . and every tongue confess that Jesus Christ is Lord" (Philippians 2:10–11).

Heavenly Father, in our weakness, give us strength, and in our foolishness, give us wisdom, so that You may be glorified. In Jesus' name we pray. Amen.

Jesus Understands Our Weakness

For we do not have a high priest who is unable to
sympathize with our weaknesses, but one who in every
respect has been tempted as we are, yet without sin.

Hebrews 4:15

This time of year is one of the most challenging for people who are on a diet. There are so many sweet treats enticing us away from our goals. We may think, "I'll just have one small bite . . ." and then before you know it, the entire plate of cookies is gone! In our weakest moments, temptation seems to be much stronger. For some, the temptation is food; for others, it may be alcohol; and for others, it may be gossip, lying, stealing, anger, and so on. We are tempted daily, and daily we will sin.

Jesus understands our weakness. He sympathizes with us and helps us in our weakest moments by giving us His strength. In 2 Corinthians 12:9, Paul writes, "But He said to me, 'My grace is sufficient for you, for My power is made perfect in weakness.' Therefore I will boast all the more gladly of my weaknesses, so that the power of Christ may rest upon me."

Though we may be tempted, we can turn to Christ in our weakness and be assured that He will give us His power to overcome it.

O Christ, so often we are tempted, just as You were. Give us strength
so that we may always do Your good and perfect will. Amen.

Take Heart

I have said these things to you, that in Me you may
have peace. In the world you will have tribulation. But
take heart; I have overcome the world.

John 16:33

This time of year, it's nice to cozy up near a fire, sip hot cocoa, and dream of peace on earth and good will toward men. But that dream quickly fades away, especially when you turn on the news and hear the reality of all that's going on in the world. We hear about earthquakes, tornadoes, murders, pandemics, protests, wars, and rumors of wars. It's hard to be at peace when so many bad things are happening all around us.

But Jesus says, "Take heart." He wants you to know that He is more powerful than all the bad news we hear about on a daily basis. Though you may face tribulation, it will not overtake you. It has no power over you because Jesus has already overcome it all. Take heart in knowing that "He who is in you is greater than he who is in the world" (1 John 4:4).

Go ahead and cozy up near the fire, sip your hot cocoa, and be at peace, knowing that God is always with you.

Dearest Jesus, give us peace in the midst of tribulation. Help us to remember that You have overcome the world and will return again to bring us to a new earth, where we will dwell with You forever. Amen.

Do the Opposite

For as by a man came death, by a man has come also
the resurrection of the dead. For as in Adam all die, so
also in Christ shall all be made alive.

1 Corinthians 15:21–22

Though this is often called the most wonderful time of year, for many, it brings only sadness. There is a technique that some people use when they are feeling down: instead of doing what they want to do, they do the opposite instead. For example, if you are sad and want to go sulk in a dark corner somewhere, instead, call a friend, or even throw a party. Doing the opposite might lift your spirits.

Through Adam, death came to all men. There is a tendency for us to still live in the old Adam, doing all the things that lead to death. The opposite of this would be to look to the man who has brought life to all. Jesus was not just a man; He was also fully God (John 10:30). He is the opposite of Adam. He is the one who came to give life.

When you feel guilt and fear that death will consume you, do the opposite. Look to Christ instead. He forgives our sins, takes away our guilt, and gives us everlasting life.

Heavenly Father, when we tend to live in the old man, help us to do the opposite and look to Your Son, who makes us new. In Him we pray. Amen.

Unfolding of Your Words

The unfolding of Your words gives light; it imparts
understanding to the simple.

Psalm 119:130

Don't you just love a good mystery? As the plot begins to thicken, we might be able to analyze the clues to predict "who done it" before it is revealed at the end. Once we see clearly, we understand, and it becomes a mystery no more.

Long before you and I were part of the world, God began to share a great mystery with the prophets of old. As His words slowly began to unfold, a great light shone brightly in the sky to lead the simple shepherds to the place where the mystery was revealed in a small stable. A Savior had been born who had come to take away the sin of the world.

On this Fourth Sunday in Advent, we light the last purple candle on our advent wreath. This final light reminds us that all the Scriptures we have heard during this season are beginning to unfold, and we can now clearly see what is about to take place. We, the simple, understand that God loved the world so much that He sent His Son, Jesus Christ, to take away our sin.

Coming Lord, may we fully understand that it is not just an entertaining story we hear this time of year but rather the unfolding of Your words, which were spoken for everyone, both then and now. Amen.

He Will Be Great

He will be great and will be called the Son of the Most
High. And the Lord God will give to Him the throne of
His father David, and He will reign over the house of
Jacob forever, and of His kingdom there will be no end.

Luke 1:32–33

What parent doesn't dream about all the wonderful possibilities their child might become one day? We imagine their potential before they are even born. We then look forward to watching them grow up, hoping and praying that they will do great things with their life.

Mary didn't have to dream or hope what her Son would become when He grew up. Our reading today is what the angel said to her when he foretold that she would conceive the Son of God. "He will be great," the angel said. Now, over two thousand years since He was born, we know that He was great in every way. He fulfilled all that He was sent to do, and now He is preparing a great and wonderful place for all those who believe in His name.

As we look forward to the upcoming celebration of the birth of our great and mighty Savior, Jesus Christ, we can sing that familiar hymn "How Great Thou Art" with full assurance that He is great and greatly to be praised.

Heavenly Father, may our celebration of Your Son's birth be a time of remembering how truly great Thou art! In His name we pray. Amen.

Possible with God

For nothing will be impossible with God.

Luke 1:37

Mary had just received some shocking news from a heavenly being. Of course, she questioned how it could be possible for her to conceive when she was still a virgin. She had to have been stunned by the notion that she would give birth to the Son of God.

The angel shares that another impossible birth is going to take place as well. Her relative Elizabeth had also conceived, even though she was barren and of old age. Both of these women trusted God and seemed to easily accept what was happening to them. Maybe because they had heard all about many other seemingly impossible events that had occurred prior to this.

From the time of creation up to the angel appearing before Mary, many impossible events have become possible with God. An elderly woman long before Elizabeth laughs when she learns that she will conceive a son; a man is swallowed by a large fish and lives, and another is thrown into a lions' den and leaves without a scratch. There are countless other incredible events such as these that leave us wondering, "How was that possible?"

How was it possible that God would love the world so much, despite our sin, that He would send His only-begotten Son to be our Savior? That's easy, because nothing is impossible with God.

Heavenly Father, give us faith to accept Your possible plans for our life. In Jesus' name we pray. Amen.

A Fulfillment

And blessed is she who believed that there would be a
fulfillment of what was spoken to her from the Lord.

Luke 1:45

"Seeing is believing" is a familiar phrase that implies that until you see something with your own eyes, you will not believe it exists. This was how Thomas thought when he heard the good news that Jesus had risen from the dead. He wanted proof before he could believe. You may recall Jesus' words to him, "Have you believed because you have seen Me? Blessed are those who have not seen and yet have believed" (John 20:29).

Unlike Thomas, Mary believed first and then patiently waited for the day she would see Jesus face to face. She believed there would be a fulfillment of all that was spoken to her. We, too, are waiting for a fulfillment of all that God has promised to those who believe in Jesus Christ. In faith, we believe, as Mary did, that Jesus had come to bring salvation to all the world. We are now waiting for the promise of His return to be fulfilled.

Without seeing, we have faith to believe that He is in heaven, preparing a place for all who believe. We believe He will return. We believe we will see Him face-to-face.

Lord Jesus Christ, give us the same faith that Mary had, so that we may believe in You as we await the fulfillment of the promise of Your return. Amen.

Do Not Be Afraid

But as he considered these things, behold, an angel of
the Lord appeared to him in a dream, saying, "Joseph,
son of David, do not fear to take Mary as your wife, for
that which is conceived in her is from the Holy Spirit."

Matthew 1:20

Mary had already been told not to be afraid. She trusted God and pondered the marvelous promise in her heart as she waited for Jesus to be born. But now it was Joseph's turn. He was contemplating what to do with the woman he was betrothed to, who was now pregnant with a child that was not his.

He was in a very complex situation, since betrothal in those days was just as binding as marriage. He had no intention of causing Mary shame, but he no longer wanted to be married to her either. He was afraid. God understood Joseph's fear and knew he was about to make a terrible mistake. Joseph needed to know that Mary had done nothing wrong. This was the work of the Holy Spirit. Sometimes, our faith is strong, and we can easily submit to God's will, as Mary had done. Sometimes, our faith requires courage when doubt seeps in and causes us to be afraid. Joseph needed courage, and the Lord provided.

Heavenly Father, help us not to be afraid during those times when we struggle to do the right thing. Give us courage to do Your will. In Your beloved Son's name we pray. Amen.

A Lowly Birth

And she gave birth to her firstborn son and wrapped
Him in swaddling cloths and laid Him in a manger,
because there was no place for them in the inn.

Luke 2:7

All that had been foretold had now come to pass. Surely God would want to announce the birth of His Son, much like they do in England with a celebratory gun salute to announce a royal birth. But instead of a royal chamber, Jesus' first cry of life was heard inside a stable. It makes no sense. Mary had been told she would give birth to a king. Why would a king have such a lowly birth?

Jesus was not sent to rule this world. He explains to Pilate after His arrest that, yes, He is a king, but this world is not His kingdom. "Jesus answered, 'My kingdom is not of this world. If My kingdom were of this world, My servants would have been fighting, that I might not be delivered over to the Jews. But My kingdom is not from the world'" (John 18:36).

King Jesus came to serve. He came to die for the forgiveness of our sins. He came to rise again, so that we might have eternal life. Though He had a lowly birth, it was a birth full of love for all mankind.

Heavenly Father, may we rejoice and celebrate that a king was born, not to condemn but to save the world. In Jesus' name we pray. Amen.

Rejoice! The Savior Was Born

For unto you is born this day in the city
of David a Savior, who is Christ the Lord.

Luke 2:11

Ah, the long-awaited Christmas morning has finally come! Regardless of what traditions your family might have for celebrating the birth of Jesus, by the end of the day, exhaustion and maybe even a little sadness sets in as you realize that another Christmas has come and gone. The thought of packing up all the decorations and then trying to find all the pine needles left behind from a dried-up Christmas tree might bring even more sadness. If only we could hold on to Christmas for just a little while longer.

Before you begin the daunting cleanup process, you should know that Christmas is not over. As a matter of fact, it's only just begun! There are still eleven more days to celebrate this truly amazing event. The long-awaited promise had finally been fulfilled. God had given us a Savior, His only Son, Jesus Christ. The announcement given to the shepherds long ago is still just as relevant and important for this generation and for all generations to come.

No, this is not a one-day celebration, or even a twelve-day celebration. This is a celebration to last your entire life. Rejoice! A Savior was born for you!

Heavenly Father, may we rejoice today and every day that in Your Son, a Savior was born to take away our sin. In His name we pray. Amen.

Treasures of the Heart

But Mary treasured up all these things,
pondering them in her heart.

Luke 2:19

While Jesus was walking among us, He said, "For where your treasure is, there your heart will be also" (Matthew 6:21). Mary knew this truth better than anyone. The shepherds had come to worship the new king, and they shared with Mary all that the angel had told them. Mary treasured these words in her heart as she held her infant son, as she cared for Him, and as she loved Him. Jesus, her precious baby boy, who was also the Savior of the world, was her greatest treasure.

What is your treasure? What do you ponder in your heart? Is it all the expensive gifts you received this year? Is it your wealth, your family, your children? What we love the most is what we treasure in our hearts the most. We have many treasures of the heart. Some are more precious than others, but none will ever be greater than the priceless treasure we received from God Himself: the free gift of salvation for all who believe in His Son, Jesus Christ.

God also treasures you in His heart. 1 Peter 2:4 says this: "As you come to Him, a living stone rejected by men but in the sight of God chosen and precious . . ."

Incarnate Word, may we, like Mary, treasure all the promises found in Your Word and ponder them daily as we await Your return. Amen.

God's Words Are True

And now, O Lord GOD, You are
God, and Your words are true.

2 Samuel 7:28

Many families read the fictional story "The Night before Christmas" to their children on Christmas Eve. It's a sweet story of a plump, rosy-cheeked, jolly old St. Nicholas, who visits the homes of all the children around the world on Christmas Eve, filling their stockings and leaving gifts under the tree. It's a story that children love to hear, and many hope it might even be true.

Then there's another story we hear at Christmas, about the birth of a baby who would one day save the world. It's also a wonderful story. However, we don't have to wonder if this story might be true or not. In our Scripture reading today, David had just received a promise from God. In gratitude, he rejoices because he knows that God's words are true.

Because we know God's words are true, we know that Jesus was born and that He walked among us. He healed the sick. He was arrested and mocked. He hung upon a cross and died, and He rose again, victorious over death. God does not lie. His words are truth, and He tells us that all who believe in His Son, Jesus Christ, will be saved and have eternal life.

Heavenly Father, may we never doubt or wonder if Your words are true. Strengthen our trust and faith so that we may always believe in Your Son, Jesus Christ. In His name we pray. Amen.

Hear and Obey

But He said, "Blessed rather are those who hear the
word of God and keep it!"

Luke 11:28

You stand very still as you look down at the scale, dreading what you might see. Sadly, once again, it tells you that you have over-indulged in your holiday feasting. No worries, you still have the diet books from last year. You just read them again and do everything they say to do. Easy, right? If so, why do so many give up after a few days?

It doesn't do anyone any good to hear and believe all the words and then lose patience in keeping them. We know that what the Bible says is true. We believe that God sent His Son, Jesus, to save us from our sin. But do we understand that we are not to continue sinning but rather to keep God's commands? The Bible is full of commands we need to hear and obey. Paul sums it up for us in Galatians 5:14: "For the whole law is fulfilled in one word: 'You shall love your neighbor as yourself.'"

Yes, it may seem hard at times to hear and obey. But God has given us His Holy Spirit to help us when we grow impatient. When we hear His Word and obey it, Jesus says we are blessed.

Heavenly Father, it's not always easy to obey Your Word. Thank You for forgiving us when we fail to do so. In Jesus' name. Amen.

Paid in Full

And you, who were dead in your trespasses and the
uncircumcision of your flesh, God made alive
together with Him, having forgiven us all our
trespasses, by canceling the record of debt that
stood against us with its legal demands. This He
set aside, nailing it to the cross.

Colossians 2:13–14

There was a lot of shopping that took place before Christmas. Maybe your preparations during Advent involved pulling out the credit card to purchase gifts, decadent foods, decorations for the lawn, and lights to make your tree twinkle. It's possible you're among the many who didn't even realize how much they were spending until the bill came in the mail. Now you wonder how it will get paid. Imagine, though, if the bill came stamped *"Paid in full."* Though you had acquired a huge debt, you owed nothing. That would be a Christmas miracle!

But seriously, who is going to pay a debt that isn't theirs to pay? Jesus came to do just that. God saw the huge debt we owed and knew we could never pay it back. In the miraculous birth of His Son, Jesus Christ, He arranged for our debt to be paid. As the nails bore deep into Jesus' hands and feet, He took His last breath and stamped *"Paid in full"* on our debt of sin.

Heavenly Father, thank You for canceling our record of debt, paying it in full when Jesus gave His life for us. In His name, hear our prayer. Amen.

He Is Faithful in All

For the word of the LORD is upright, and all His work
is done in faithfulness.

Psalm 33:4

At some point in all of our lives, we have made a vow, or a promise, to God or others. If you were confirmed in the faith, you made a promise to be faithful to Christ all the days of your life. If you are married, during the marriage ceremony, you made a promise to be faithful to your spouse. Based on the divorce rate and the drop in church attendance, I think it is fair to say that we do not always keep our vows or promises.

This is not the case with God. Every single promise God has made in Holy Scripture He has kept. He is faithful in all He has said He will do. He promised us a Savior. He fulfilled that promise by sending His own Son, Jesus Christ. He promised to always be with us. He fulfilled that promise by sending the Holy Spirit. Jesus promised He would return again and bring us to live with Him for all eternity. Though this has not yet happened, in faith, we believe it will, because He is faithful. He has proven this to us time after time.

Heavenly Father, though You are always faithful, we are not, and we often break the promises we have made to You and others. Forgive us and help us to be Your faithful followers. In Christ Jesus' name we pray. Amen.

In the Beginning

In the beginning was the Word, and the
Word was with God, and the Word was God.
He was in the beginning with God.

John 1:1–2

Every story has a beginning, a middle, and an end. In the story of Jesus' birth, the main characters were Joseph, Mary, the angels, and later, the shepherds. Of course, the main character was Jesus Christ Himself. Often, we think of Jesus' birth as the beginning of His story. But this is not where His story begins. For that, we have to go all the way back to the very beginning of time.

In Genesis 1:1, we read that "in the beginning, God created the heavens and the earth." In our reading today, we also read that "in the beginning was the Word." In John 1:14, we read that "the Word became flesh and dwelt among us." The Word is Jesus, and He was there in the very beginning. He was there in the middle, and He will be there at the end when He returns again.

We all love a happy ending, don't we? But what about a happy beginning? Knowing that our Savior was there from the very beginning of time is comforting to us as we await His promised return.

Heavenly Father, we look forward with hope to the happily ever after that will be given to all those who believe in Your Son. Thank You for always being with us. Amen.

He Was Called Jesus

And at the end of eight days, when He was
circumcised, He was called Jesus, the name given by
the angel before He was conceived in the womb.

Luke 2:21

Sometimes if a child is born in December, he or she will be given a name associated with the season, like *Holly, Noel,* or *Nicholas.* We often give our children names that will remind us of the time when they were born. Parents may also look at meanings first to decide on the perfect name for their child. Jesus' name is also a description of who He is—He is our Savior.

Jesus received His name when Joseph and Mary brought the newborn Son of God to the temple to be circumcised. Mary had been given the name *Jesus* by God's messenger before she even conceived, and surely she had been pondering its meaning in her heart ever since. "She will bear a son, and you shall call His name Jesus, for He will save His people from their sins" (Matthew 1:21).

Our promised Savior fulfilled every prophesy that had been foretold about Him. To this day, the purpose of His name has not changed. He is still the Savior of the world, and all those who call upon His holy and precious name shall be saved.

Heavenly Father, we are grateful that Your name has a meaning that is so important to each of us. You are our promised Savior. In Jesus' holy name we pray. Amen.

My Eyes Have Seen

For my eyes have seen Your salvation.

Luke 2:30

Did you get what you wanted for Christmas this year? Or did you have to force a smile as you unwrapped another tie you didn't need or a sweater that was two sizes too small? Every now and then, you might receive a gift that surprises you. Though you didn't ask for it, once you see it, you instantly know that it is the perfect gift. These are the best kind of gifts.

A devout and righteous man named Simeon was waiting for such a gift. The Holy Spirit had promised him that he would see the Messiah before he died. Simeon waited a very long time, but when his eyes beheld Jesus for the first time, he instantly knew the waiting was over. As he held Jesus in his arms, he could do nothing else but praise God for His faithfulness.

We, like Simeon, can say with full assurance, "My eyes have seen Your salvation." We see it every time a child is brought to the baptismal font. We see it when a person repents and turns from sin. We see it in our own lives as we turn to Christ in faith and receive His surprising gift of salvation, given to all who believe.

Heavenly Father, may we always see with clarity the salvation You freely give to those who believe. We praise You for this precious gift. Through Jesus Christ, our Lord. Amen.

A Pierced Soul

(And a sword will pierce through your
own soul also), so that thoughts from
many hearts may be revealed.

Luke 2:35

When a young child has been hurt, he will often run crying to his mother with outstretched arms. Minor cuts and scrapes are easily kissed away, but if there is a serious injury, his mother might wish she could take the pain and suffering upon herself so her child doesn't have to.

Of all the prophesies Mary had been given regarding Jesus, this one had to have been the hardest to hear. Not only would her son suffer, but she, too, would feel the pain. Mary could do nothing more than watch and pray as she stood at the cross. As the spear pierced Jesus' side, she felt the stabbing pain of a pierced soul.

At times, we, too, have a pierced soul. The guilt and shame of our sins stab deep into our hearts and minds, causing pain, suffering, and despair. At such times, we can be comforted by what happened for us when Jesus died upon the cross. "He Himself bore our sins in His body on the tree, that we might die to sin and live to righteousness. By His wounds you have been healed" (1 Peter 2:24).

O Christ, often we are consumed with the piercing guilt of our sin. Forgive us, we pray, and remind us that it was Your wounds that bring healing to ours. Amen.

Where Is the King?

Now after Jesus was born in Bethlehem of Judea in the
days of Herod the king, behold, wise men from the east
came to Jerusalem, saying, "Where is He who has been
born king of the Jews? For we saw His star when it rose
and have come to worship Him."

Matthew 2:1–2

There are so many things we don't know about the Wise Men.
Were there really only three of them? Did they witness Jesus' birth, as
our nativity sets would suggest? Were they actually kings, as our children's programs make them out to be? We don't have all the answers,
but we do know that the Wise Men were searching for a king.

Though they found King Herod, they knew he was not the king
they were searching for. They wanted to find the infant who had been
born king of the Jews. The star was their guide, and following the sign
they had been given, they eventually came to the home where Jesus
lived, and there they worshiped Him.

Though we don't have a star to point us to Jesus as the Wise Men
did, we do have His Word as a light to guide us to the King of kings
and Lord of lords (1 Timothy 6:15) so that we, too, may worship Him.

Dearest Jesus, grant us Your Holy Spirit, so that we might remain
steadfast in faith, seeking first Your kingdom with as much determi-
nation as the Wise Men did. Amen.

We Were Told

They told him, "In Bethlehem of Judea, for so it is
written by the prophet."

Matthew 2:5

It's hard to find something if you have no idea where to even begin to look for it. Wouldn't it be nice if you had a map showing you exactly where the missing item was located? Kind of like a pirate's map with a bold, red *X* to mark the exact spot. Thankfully, when it comes to spiritual matters, we do have such a map: God's Holy Word.

Herod was surprised when the Wise Men appeared searching for a new king. He had not been told of this birth. He brought together the priests and teachers of the Law and asked where this new king of the Jews could be found. They didn't even hesitate when they answered, because God had clearly marked the spot! He's in Bethlehem!

God's Word is not just a book of fictional stories. It is a trustworthy map that leads us to Jesus, our Savior. We were told by the prophets where Jesus would be born. We were told how He would suffer and die for our sins. We were told that He would raise from the dead. We were told that He returned to heaven to prepare a place for us, and we are told He will return again.

Heavenly Father, how grateful we are that You told us You would
send the Holy Spirit so that You would always be with us. Amen.

Gifts for a King

And going into the house, they saw the child with
Mary His mother, and they fell down and worshiped
Him. Then, opening their treasures, they offered Him
gifts, gold and frankincense and myrrh.

Matthew 2:11

Today marks the last day of Christmas. It is also Epiphany, the day we celebrate the Wise Men finally finding Jesus and presenting Him with gifts appropriate for a king. Throughout the Scriptures, we learn about the gifts that Jesus gave to us, the most important being the gift of salvation. How are we to respond to such gracious gifts?

Paul writes in Romans 11:34–36, "For who has known the mind of the Lord, or who has been His counselor? Or who has given a gift to Him that he might be repaid? For from Him and through Him and to Him are all things." It's evident that God already has everything. What more could He possibly want? If you read a little further, Paul writes, "I appeal to you therefore, brothers, by the mercies of God, to present your bodies as a living sacrifice, holy and acceptable to God, which is your spiritual worship" (Romans 12:1).

God wants all of you, not just a part. This is how, in faith, we respond to our Savior and King, Jesus Christ.

Heavenly Father, we once again give You thanks and praise for giving us Your Son, Jesus Christ. Grant us Your Holy Spirit that we may remain steadfast in faith, living to Your glory, through Him who reigns with You and the Holy Spirit. Amen.